This book is dedicated in memory of two great men who devoted their lives to helping their neighbors. Vice Admiral Jack Fetterman and former Pensacola, Florida, Mayor Vince Whibbs both lived life to the fullest. Though they are no longer with us, their stories will continue to inspire residents of Pensacola every day.

~ Quint Studer

ISBN-13: 978-0-9791103-0-6
ISBN-10: 0-9791103-0-0

Printed in the United States by Boyd Printing.

Panama City, Florida, USA

Making a Difference

Years ago, I asked my hospital staff, "How can we improve the patient's satisfaction with the level of care?"

Some replied that it wasn't always possible, particularly if the patient is in pain or he has been given bad news. One staff member asked, "How can we make him feel good under those circumstances?"

Covenant Hospice does it all the time. Their motto is "add life to days when days can no longer be added to life." More and more healthcare professionals have adopted this as their daily mantra. It has literally changed how so many of us look at healthcare today.

Covenant Hospice professionals are truly making a difference each and every day. Their success stories are too numerous to capture in any one book or in this brief foreword. They help patients and their loved ones come to peace with the next phase of life. As you look through these pages, realize that behind each picture is a story of acceptance and love.

And remember, Covenant Hospice is about people—always has been, always will be.

Quint Studer

Covenant Hospice is grateful to healthcare professional, author, and speaker Quint Studer for his support of Faces of Life. Inc. Magazine *named Quint its Master of Business, the only healthcare leader to ever receive this distinction. Quint's first book,* Hardwiring Excellence, *was published in 2004 and is already in its sixth printing of 100,000 copies.*

Faces of Life

life is not about how you die, but how you live

In celebration of National Hospice Month in November of 2005, we created *Faces of Life*. A powerful exhibit of photographs and inspiring stories from our patients and families, the stories told of hope and life, of the human spirit, and of living each day to its fullest.

The goal of the exhibit was to celebrate life's journey. At Covenant Hospice, we feel that the end of life is not about how you die, but how you live.

Because of the exhibit's great success, this year we decided to take the project a step farther and publish stories and photographs in a hardbound book. By purchasing this collection, you are supporting Covenant Hospice. We are a not-for-profit organization dedicated to providing comprehensive, compassionate service to patients and loved ones during times of life-limiting illnesses. Our care is always based on need, not the ability to pay.

We consider it an honor to be a part of the lives of our patients and families. We hope you find these stories to be inspirational and encourage you to add life to your days while positively impacting those around you, like all of the people in this book have done. After all, it's all about living.

Our Stories...

Juan

Juan's Determination

he built his legacy with his own two hands

At the end of his life, Juan spent all of his free time helping Habitat for Humanity construct new houses for his neighbors. He took on this strenuous work because his dying wish was to make certain that his wife, Maria, and their young grandson, Carlos, would live in a nice home once he was gone. Juan had liver cancer.

After spending his last seven months contributing the grueling 300 hours of volunteer work called "sweat equity" that qualified his family for a Habitat home of their own, Juan passed in peace knowing that he had ensured his family would have a home. He built his legacy with his own two hands.

Now, although Juan is no longer with them, Maria and Carlos have something to look forward to. They will be moving into their new home soon. Maria can't wait to plant a garden in her new yard. When she moves in, Maria will remember that as Juan built other Habitat homes, he would pick up his rake or broom and would dance with it because he was so happy that he was providing for his family. Then, she will smile.

A humble man who learned to depend on God during his battle with cancer; Juan always looked forward to seeing George Morgan, Covenant Hospice chaplain, for anointment, communion and blessing. Maria wants people to remember her husband as a man who was determined to help others and taught his grandson to be a good person.

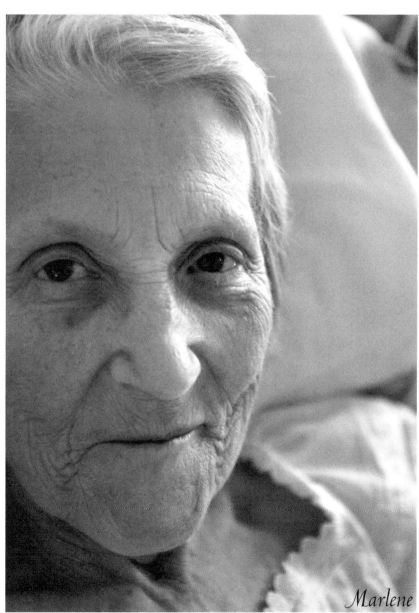

Marlene

Marlene's Freedom

Novelist and mother of three Maria 'Marlene' Magdal Patterson is thankful for something that most people take for granted: Since she survived World War II while living under Hitler's rule in Austria, freedom is precious to her. Her novel, *In the Claws of the Vulture*, tells the story of her childhood in Austria during the War. In the book, she describes the fears and trials that she and her neighbors experienced and how she faced that trying time head-on and positively.

Now, Marlene is facing another trying time with positivity: She is battling breast cancer. While she isn't afraid to die, she does wish that she didn't have to be separated from her children and grandchildren.

Marlene's positive outlook has helped her own children as well as many others throughout her community. When she presented *In the Claws of the Vulture* in area schools, Maria told the children: "A person should never, ever, ever give up. No matter what today looks like, there is always a better, clearer day coming."

With loads of friends and family who sometimes travel hundreds of miles just to spend a few moments with her, Marlene is happy. Her best friend of 30 years, June, has made daily visits to be at her side, making it clear that she will be there until the end. Whenever June helps her to complete a task, Marlene apologizes, only to hear June ask, "Would you do the same for me?" Maria knows that their friendship is truly a two-way street.

Above all, Marlene feels that her greatest accomplishment in life was having the freedom to be a missionary in Eastern Europe. "I think the thing I am most proud of is the fact that I was a woman by myself going behind the Iron Curtain, serving people who needed help." Her pioneering accomplishments speak volumes about what will be her legacy: "I would like the world to know that I was a person who was able to stand on my feet and say that this is who I am, this is where I stand, this is my opinion, this is what I stand for."

Sarah's Roots

Sarah Terrell was born May 4, 1906, in Lower Peachtree, Alabama, and from the moment of her birth, was the epitome of a Southern woman. She had a strong faith, attended church, was an excellent homemaker and loved to cook. Her favorite part of cooking was feeding others. Anytime her family or friends came to visit, they couldn't leave her house without a plate full of her fine, Southern cuisine. Her grandniece Sharon Darrington says, "She would have you eat at every visit—even if you told her you had just eaten. She would cook the best soul food such as fried chicken, collard greens, and biscuits. She would cook for you even if it took hours to prepare!"

When Sharon was attending Bishop State Community College, she frequently visited her Aunt Sarah. On one visit, Sarah "was cooking green beans, and I did not like green beans at all," Sharon remembers. "Sarah kept on telling me that they were good for me, so finally after her pressuring me to eat them, I ate them. Now, I love beans!" Sarah always wanted people to try different foods.

An avid reader, Sarah loved to read to children and promote their interest in reading. She read anything and everything, even the tiny print on each of her medicine prescriptions. She wanted to know every little thing about those medicines.

Sarah became ill and was under the care of Covenant Hospice when she passed away at 99 years old. Her family says that they will remember her as a strong, independent woman with a Southern sweetness. They think it was all of those qualities that enabled her to live such a long life. As a Covenant Hospice employee, Sharon is proud to carry on Sarah's Southern roots.

Garrett

Steven's Purpose

On July 12, 2005, just two days after Hurricane Dennis, Tammy Morgan, her son Steven, and her parents went for a swim in their backyard pool. As many children do, Steven was trying to see how long he could hold his breath underwater while trying to swim the length of the pool and back, which he had done so many times in the past. That day, Steven suffered from shallow water blackout and lost his life at the young age of 13. Shallow water blackout is a sudden unconsciousness that can occur with over-hyperventilation and breath holding.

After his death, Steven's parents and family sought Covenant Hospice for bereavement services, which are available for free to anyone in the community. "Our family took advantage of this service, and the help we received has been invaluable," said Tammy.

Steven lived life like an adventure and was known to many as "Stevil-Knievel." His passion was sports, especially skateboarding. Tammy says her son was funny, determined, focused and adventurous. "Steven could think outside the box," she said.

One of Steven's best friends, Garrett, is carrying on the dream of his late friend. Garrett is selling t-shirts in Steven's memory to raise money for a community-proposed skate park in Milton, Florida. He has already raised $2,500, which he plans to donate to the city to help fund the new skate park in honor of his best friend.

Garrett's work for the park shows that Steven's legacy is already impacting people. "Each day he woke up with a purpose—projects to complete and new challenges to tackle," says his mom. Steven's motto in life and what he frequently told his parents was "Fear is not an option." Today, his family is busy spreading the word about shallow water blackout. "Hopefully this knowledge will help save a life," said Tammy.

Rubin

Rubin's Generosity

Rubin loved people. As a businessman in Manhattan for several years, he was known for how much he valued his employees and customers, how he nurtured them and treated them well. If someone needed something, all they had to do was ask, and Rubin would give it to them.

Late in life, he moved from the city to upstate New York and bought a farm where he gardened, fished and bred horses. He never lost his city accent, though, and when he spoke, people knew immediately that he was a New Yorker. Then after relocating to Niceville, Florida, Rubin had to get used to a Covenant Hospice Home Health Aid's Southern accent. He loved her and nicknamed her "Alabama."

Throughout his life in Manhattan, upstate New York and Northwest Florida, Rubin's hobbies of painting and baseball kept him busy. His folksy paintings graced his room at his daughter Becky's house. He was fascinated with Native American art and mimicked the style. He also painted several small silhouettes of Charlie Chaplin. He watched Babe Ruth play at Yankee Stadium, and he greatly admired the talents and dedication of Gehrig and DiMaggio. He delighted at the memory of Lazzeri and Crosetti turning a double play. "They were the best," he would say.

As an Orthodox Jew, whenever Rubin parted ways with someone, he would say, "Shalom...and God bless."

Rubin loved his family; he was generous to them and to all who came to know him.

Shalom, Rubin...and God bless.

Susan

Meagan's Music

After losing her daughter Meagan, Susan Campbell had no idea she could ever be a 'normal' person again. But through the love and support of her family and Covenant Hospice, she was able to form a new 'normal' and go on with her life as a wife and mother.

Meagan was living her dream. She was a freshman at Flagler College in St. Augustine, Florida, and was planning to try out for the Flagler Women's Golf Team. But on Friday, September 13, 2002, Meagan was driving home from college for the first time when she was involved in a multi-car accident that took her life. "We were devastated, in complete shock. This wasn't supposed to happen to us. What were we going to do without our Meagan?" asked Susan.

Each of her family members shared a love of something with Meagan. She shared the love of golf and competition with her dad, the love of sushi with her brother Ryan, and the love of music with her mom.

"Through Meagan's love of music, God gave us comfort after her death," explains Susan. "Each year our city has the Boggy Bayou Mullet Festival. Several popular music groups perform. Meagan loved the Mullet Festival. In October 2001, she had the opportunity to go backstage to meet one of her favorite country groups, Diamond Rio. She was so excited that she forgot to bring something for autographs, so she pulled out a $5 bill and had each member sign it."

"For Meagan, this was such a special night. At the time, we didn't realize how important this night would be in our lives; but now we know. This blessing became apparent a few months after Meagan died. Talk about timing being everything—my heart was aching, so when I heard the song "I Believe," I dropped to my knees, cried and prayed. It was as if Meagan was letting me know she is in a better place, living a grander life than ever. This song helped me regain my faith in God. I needed God to help me with my pain. Two other Diamond Rio songs that have influenced me are "One More Day," for the days I long to have Meagan with me, and "God Only Cries for the Living." This song reminds me that through God's love there is a heavenly place, and I will one glorious day be with my Meagan again!" exclaims Susan.

Until then, Susan plans to volunteer in Covenant Hospice's Bereavement Department to help other families who have lost children.

George

George's Son

nothing could change the way we felt about him

George and his wife had no way of knowing when they brought their infant son home that they'd be losing him at such a young age. Ken died of AIDS at the age of 33 in Room 3 at the Joyce Goldenberg Hospice Inpatient Residence in Pensacola, Florida.

When Ken entered high school, his parents noticed that he didn't date many girls. "When my son told us he was homosexual, I told him that we raised him, loved him, and that nothing could change the way we felt about him," George states.

As Ken's disease progressed, it became clear that hospice would be the only option. "My first priority from the get-go was making sure my son received the best care possible," says George.

As a retired law enforcement officer of 38 years, George felt that he could trust local physicians and medical staff to care for his son. He prides himself on being able to read people based on his past experience. "I can tell sincerity when I see it," he says. He found that with the Covenant Hospice staff.

Ken passed away in 1997. George had him cremated, scattered half of his ashes in the Gulf and placed the other half in a cemetery near his mother's home in Milton, Florida. In April 2004, George found his way back to Covenant Hospice.

"Something struck me," George explains, "I felt like I needed to do something."

George volunteers at the Goldenberg Residence every Thursday. He takes out the garbage, makes coffee, and sits with patients or families when requested. He is honored to share his son's story and comfort grieving family members with the knowledge that his son received top-notch care.

George has no regrets about his son's final days. He feels that the staff "always did the right thing." He just feels that now it's his turn to give something back. "The more I am here, the more I feel like I need to contribute. I just can't see myself not doing something for the special people here."

Alison

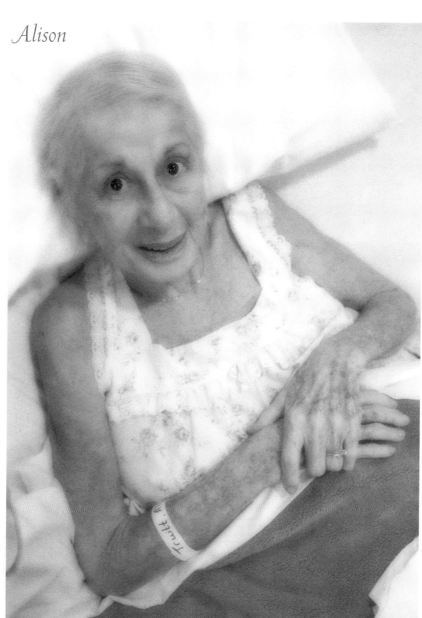

Photo by Look Who Just Blouin Photography

Alison's Elegance

Alison Truitt has traveled all over the world—from her birthplace, Paris, France, to various countries in Europe and every state in the U.S. Her favorite places were Brazil, London, and, of course, her hometown: She loved Paris' art and culture.

Before settling down and having children, Alison's adventurous life included acting on the big screen and rubbing elbows with the likes of Tom Boswell, also known as Mr. Cunningham on *Happy Days*. When Alison became pregnant with her first child, she packed her bags and left the jet-setting Hollywood scene. She headed to Key West, Florida, a mecca for culture and arts and a place that reminded her of Paris. While living in Key West, Alison ran an art gallery in the artists' colony.

Alison raised her three children on her own, all the while remaining poised and elegant. Her children are all grown up now and spread out: One lives in North Carolina, the other two in Florida. Alison is extremely proud of them all and feels they are very successful. The love her children have for their mother is evident when you walk into her room at the Covenant Hospice Inpatient and Palliative Care Center at West Florida Hospital. Cards and flowers fill the room, the way they did when there was a big star with her name on the door.

Even as she battles a terminal illness, Alison remains elegant and graceful. Many of the nursing staff flock to her room to hear stories about her travels, art, and her life experiences. She can still captivate an audience and does so often at the Care Center. Some days, she even has her hair and makeup done—just like she did when she was in the movies.

Joyce & Sam

Joyce's Contributions

wrapped in her arms' warmth and comfort

After retiring from being in business with her husband, Sam, for 40 years, Joyce Goldenberg looked into volunteering for various local nonprofits. Taking the advice of a friend, Joyce attended a volunteer training program with Covenant Hospice and enjoyed her training so much that she decided to become a new patient and family volunteer. "I did not know anything about hospice at first, but I learned about caring for the sick and elderly early on from my mother and my grandmother," she says.

When Joyce heard that Covenant Hospice was building an inpatient residence, she knew that she had to be a part of it. In the spring of 1992, Joyce became the first patient and family volunteer at the new residence. Throughout the years, Joyce has grown attached to many patients and experienced the pain of loss when they passed away. "I loved them all," she says of the patients she has cared for. Even though these patients have moved on, Joyce remembers their stories clearly, and a smile appears on her face as she looks back.

Joyce remembers Betty, a patient who enjoyed making dolls. Recognizing Betty's attachment to the craft, Joyce received permission to take Betty to a local nursing home where she instructed residents on how to make their own dolls. "I can't tell you how much that meant to Betty to be able to share her skills with others," Joyce says.

She also remembers a time when she asked a male patient, in the final hours of his life, if she could get him anything. The elderly man said, "I want my mama." Knowing that wasn't possible, Joyce did what she could: She cradled the man in her arms and began to rock him. "Mama is here," she said. The man passed away wrapped in her arms' warmth and comfort.

A young AIDS patient left a loving impression upon Joyce. During hospice's traditional tree trimming, the patient's partner brought matching engraved ornaments. Once his partner's ornament was placed, the patient turned to Joyce and told her that he wanted her to place his ornament on the tree. Joyce tried to find several branches to support the ornament, but had difficulty. Finally, she placed the ornament on a branch next to his partner's. It sat on the limb perfectly, as if the ornaments were meant to be together.

Joyce has been impacted in many ways by her patients, learning from them "to die with dignity and in comfort." Joyce's contributions to Covenant Hospice include the many lives she has touched, as well as her continued love and dedication. She is responsible for creating and organizing an annual garage sale, which, over the past 11 years, has raised more than one million dollars. And to recognize their mother, Joyce's children presented a monetary gift to Covenant Hospice. The sign outside the building where she continues to volunteer now reads "The Joyce Goldenberg Inpatient Residence." Although she never set out to, Joyce Goldenberg, with Sam supporting her, has truly become the face of Covenant Hospice.

Little Robbie

Big Robbie's Legacy

me and my daddy sat together

Known to many as Big Robbie, Robert Busby, Sr.'s favorite things were working out, riding motorcycles and spending time with his family, especially his six-year-old son, Robert Busby, Jr. or Little Robbie. Little Robbie shared some things about his daddy with a Covenant Hospice children's bereavement specialist.

Tell us about your daddy.
"He was a nice daddy. He would teach me about anything he was doing. Me and my daddy sat together every morning watching *Dora the Explorer*."

Share some fun times you had with your daddy.
"I would follow Daddy everywhere he went. When he was doing push-ups, I would climb on his back. He would ride me on the motorcycle every time he went somewhere. I liked being with my daddy and feeling the wind."

What lessons did your daddy teach you?
"Never hit girls. Go to church. Don't tell lies. Read our Bible."

Did your daddy teach you how to do things?
"He taught me how to ride my bike and how to do sit-ups and how to unscrew things and put them back together and how to swim."

What do you remember about your daddy?
"He always had a smile on his face."

Big Robbie battled brain cancer and was under the care of Covenant Hospice. Even though his life was shorter than expected, the moments that Big Robbie spent with his family and the positive impact that he had on their lives will always be cherished. Through Little Robbie, his legacy will live on for generations.

Richard

Richard's Bravery

you can do anything

Richard Tharps' Service Station, Tharps & Sons, wasn't just a place to fill up your car with gasoline. Rather, it was a place where people would laugh, where enemies would become friends and where they could get food for their soul. The station was known to many in the town of Dothan, Alabama, and Richard Tharps is thought of fondly in the area.

Richard opened Tharps & Sons in the early 1960s when the Ku Klux Klan bombed Sixteenth Street Baptist Church in Birmingham, Alabama, killing four young girls; when Joseph McNeill was leading the sit-in campaigns at Woolworth's in Greensboro, North Carolina; and when Dr. Martin Luther King, Jr. gave his "I Have a Dream" speech in Washington, DC. It was a time of civil unrest and hatred in our country. When Richard opened Tharps & Sons, he became the second African American business owner in the Dothan area. By bravely opening his business, his daughter Cedalia says, "It showed others that with faith in God and determination, you can do anything."

Owning his own business took up most of his days, but Richard found time to be a wonderful father. "On Saturdays, I would go to work with him, and he would teach me the ins and outs of managing a business, and on Sunday afternoons, he taught me how to two-step in the living room," says Cedalia. Richard instilled a great work ethic in Cedalia. After all, he opened the business at 7 am and closed it at 9 pm—14 hour days!

Richard touched the lives of so many in the Dothan community. It was his bravery that provided a place of friendship and fellowship that was truly a blessing for many who came to fill up their tanks and their souls.

C.O.Z.'s Present

On her 104th birthday, C.O.Z. Peterson got something that she had been wishing for her whole life. As a birthday present, the Florida State Attorney's Office prosecutor, Joe Grammer, presented C.O.Z. with an honorary state attorney award. She always wanted to be an attorney, but her mother discouraged it. "That was my greatest ambition," she said as she accepted the award.

C.O.Z. was raised outside of Marianna, Florida, and was married at 17 according to her mother's wishes. She met her husband at church. "Back then, the church was the courting ground," she says. C.O.Z. didn't have any children of her own, but she did raise her three nieces and one nephew.

Longevity is in C.O.Z.'s blood. Her grandfather, born in Africa, lived to be 115 and earned his freedom from slavery. "When I was a little girl, I used to love going to my grandfather's house. He would tell us stories about Africa and the trip over to America on a slave ship," she says. He told her of how they crossed the "big water," what he did as a slave in Florida, and then how he ultimately reunited with his sisters and brothers when slavery was abolished.

Covenant Hospice's Faith in Action Volunteer Program takes care of non-hospice patients like C.O.Z. who are frail, sick, and elderly but not terminally ill. After hearing C.O.Z. express her desire to be an attorney, a Covenant Hospice employee had the idea to make that possible.

As C.O.Z. sits in her chair reflecting on her life and this new dream that she achieved, she says that the happiest time in her life is now. She's realized that she has done the best she can in life, and she has no wants or needs. She is proud of her major accomplishments such as raising her brother's children and maintaining her memory for 104 years.

C.O.Z. has learned—from her grandfather's life and her own—to do unto mankind as we would desire them to do unto us. She thinks this is the greatest present you can give someone.

Ruth and Bill

Photo by Look Who Just Blouin Photography

Ruth & Bill's Connection

they shared an instant connection

Ruth Sanborn was born in Medford, Massachusetts. Her graduating senior class totaled 787 people. Bill Sanborn, on the other hand, grew up in a small town in New Hampshire with a graduating high school class of only 11 people.

Bill loves to talk about the small country town where he grew up. He attributes Epping, New Hampshire, with giving him a passion for growing flowers and vegetables. He even studied horticulture at the University of New Hampshire. Bill tragically lost his first wife to cancer; it was an extremely tough time for him. But then he met Ruth.

Ruth, executive director of the Housing Authority in Exeter, New Hampshire, lost her first husband to alcoholism. Later, some friends of Ruth, 57, and Bill, 58, decided to set the two up on a blind date. They were both very nervous to go on a date, but when they finally went for a nice dinner, they shared an instant connection.

A few months later, Bill decided, without consulting Ruth, to announce to everyone at a family gathering that they were getting married. Lucky for him, Ruth was thrilled with the idea. Throughout their 28 years of marriage, Ruth battled many health problems, but Bill was there every step of the way. Ruth said, "I told him he already had his wings—all he had to do would be to put on the halo." Bill felt so lucky to be married to a wonderful lady and to be like a father to Ruth's son and daughter. "I even got to give her daughter away at her wedding," he said. They were surrounded by lots of love from Ruth's two children and Bill's three sons.

Bill and Ruth passed away within a day of each other under Covenant Hospice's care. They died the same way they lived—together.

Albert

Photo by Mattox Studio

Albert's Travels

At age 93, author Albert Thon has many chapters in his book of life. He has traveled the world, including every state in the Union except Alaska and has been to every country in Europe west of the Rhine River. For him, the happiest times in his life were when he was boarding a plane.

Albert's first trip to Europe was in 1967 and his last was in 1998, when he drove a car from Paris to Madrid and then to Barcelona, Spain. He prefers to travel alone: "That way I can do what I want when I want to do it." However, he has been known to take friends along with him on various trips.

Albert's many journeys to Europe prompted him to write his first book, *Gramercy Park*. In addition to *Gramercy Park*, he has also penned three other novels that you can find for sale on the Internet. His other works include *Napoleon's Secret Army*, *Every House Has Its Secrets* and *If Booth Had Missed*. The books range from murder mystery novels to political satire, but he is most proud of *Gramercy Park*. "I never lived over in Europe, but I think I did a good job of capturing that culture," says Albert.

Albert's greatest personal accomplishment in life is that he never touched alcohol or tobacco, and he says, "I reaped the benefits of my lifestyle." He credits this "clean living" for making it possible to write his novels and travel the world. He will tell you it made his life richer. Throughout his life, he has seen friends develop "bad habits" with alcohol and tobacco, from which he developed his motto: "You pay for every mistake you make in life."

The life lesson that Albert likes to share with everyone is "to be moderate in all things," unless, of course, it involves traveling or writing.

Tom

Tom's Children

When parents took their children to Dr. Tom Jenkins, they knew that he was giving each of them all of the time, devotion and compassion they deserved. Dr. Jenkins wasn't just a doctor, he was a friend to the children he cared for. As a board certified pediatric oncologist and hematologist, he spent 30 years caring for children with terminal illnesses, and he learned all of their names. When he saw his patients—his children—in public, he took the time to call them by name and chat with them.

In 2004, Tom died of cancer, the same disease that he had treated in many of his patients. As a doctor and a patient, Tom's colleagues described him as always precise, caring and thorough. He embraced his practice of medicine to the fullest, as he did most things in life.

One night in his youth, Tom begrudgingly went on a blind date and ended up meeting his wife, Penny, who, it turned out, hadn't wanted to go on the date either! But as fate would have it, they fell in love and were married for 36 years. Penny wasn't quite sure if she wanted to marry a man with such a demanding job, but Tom's passion for life reeled her in. They had a daughter and a son, and even though life was hectic, Tom always found time for his family. Sometimes Penny would take the children and wait for him in one of his exam rooms. For the Jenkins family, it didn't matter where they spent time together, all that mattered was being together.

Penny describes Tom as a quiet, supportive and caring man, someone who was private and unassuming. "He loved learning and wanted to help someone everyday of his life," she explains. When doctors discovered Tom's brain tumor, and Tom knew he had to stop seeing patients, the frustration of not being able to help children weighed heavily on him. Determined to continue helping patients, he would sit in on Friday rounds at Nemours Children's Clinic in Pensacola, Florida, so that he could be indirectly involved with aiding children.

Tom taught his own children many things. Penny says with a chuckle, "When our children would ask him questions, Tom was sure to give them very in-depth answers whether they wanted them or not." Tom also taught his family what it meant to be a good parent and husband. He emphasized the need and significance of communication in relationships. Simply put, he passed his passion for life onto his family, showing them how to embrace love and live their lives to the fullest.

Minnie

Photo by Look Who Just Blouin Photography

Minnie's Touch

It is hard to say how many two-legged and four-legged friends Minnie has made in her lifetime, but one thing is for sure: In her 94 years, she has touched the lives of countless people with her humor, remarkable spirit, and gracious ways.

Minnie has a wonderful legacy with her family. She married when she was 13 years old, raised three daughters during the Depression, traveled when she was younger, and worked in housekeeping and school cafeterias. There, she made many wonderful impressions with her delicious cooking; something her family readily attests to! Minnie remembers the day the Japanese surrendered and how people dropped what they were doing to celebrate in the streets, and then in the next breath relates how wonderful her great-grandchildren are, and how she has had a good life.

So her daughter Margaret could better care for her, Minnie moved from her beloved Meridian, Mississippi, to Mobile, Alabama, in 2005. Though her health continues to decline and family roles have shifted, Minnie retains her independent spirit as best she can. Warm visits from Covenant's 'Paws for Patients' therapy dog, Mela, fill her days with comfort and help rekindle that spirit she had put on the shelf after leaving her home in Mississippi. After Mela's first visit, Minnie suddenly decided that she "needed to get out of her room more," maybe get her nails done, talk with the other residents, attend church services, or go to the dining room to check on the cooking. Just as she has touched others, Mela has touched her.

Diane

June's Adventure

June Cleveland was Diane Harvey's devoted Girl Scout leader for eight years. She led Diane's troop from Brownies through Senior Scouts and equipped the girls in every way possible, teaching them how to knit, embroider and mend. She also taught them camping skills, first aid, social skills, and perseverance.

June began Diane and the girls' camping experience in her living room. When they got really good, they advanced to cabins, tents, and finally primitive camping—even though as girls they were not very happy with the lack of amenities. Two of June's favorite places to take the girls were Scoutshire Woods in Alabama and Audubon Park in New Orleans.

The culmination of June's scouting career was the troop's three-week adventure to the New York World's Fair in 1964. In the 1960s, not many people from Diane's small town of Mobile, Alabama made the 1,200-mile trek to New York City, so this was a huge accomplishment for June and for the girls in the troop.

For two entire years, June and the girls raised money for the trip. In order to drive all the way to the Big Apple, they had to raise some big bucks. So, they had rummage sale after rummage sale, fish fries, spaghetti dinners, doughnut sales and of course the famous Girl Scout cookie sales! After June and her troop finally raised enough money, they traveled by bus from Mobile up the east coast, stopping at places along the way like Savannah, Jamestown, and Williamsburg. June wanted to make an adventure out of their long road trip.

When the troop got to the Big Apple, they could not believe all of the huge skyscrapers they saw as they came across the bridge. Growing up in Mobile, they had never seen anything like that. In New York, the troop attended the World's Fair and saw all the sights—the Empire State Building, the Statue of Liberty and Greenwich Village. June and the girls also got to sit in the audience of the game show "Beat the Clock" with Bud Collier. Since June wanted to teach the girls how to be real Girl Scouts and have them use the skills she taught them, they camped out on Long Island instead of staying in a luxury hotel.

The trip didn't end in the Big Apple. The troop visited Philadelphia, Washington, DC and other cities. While in DC, June even arranged for the troop to have lunch in the Capitol with Alabama Senator, John Sparkman.

June passed away December 18, 2005. Diane says, "Each day I work at Covenant Hospice as a bereavement specialist, I carry with me the love and patience that June instilled in me as a Girl Scout and how she inspired a love of adventure in all us girls. June, my 'second mom,' touched my life forever."

Gladys

Gladys's Gifts

would not settle for anything less than the best

If the value of a life were measured in the gifts we give to others, then Gladys would be wealthy beyond belief.

Gladys was a young wife with two girls and two boys when her husband died unexpectedly. Forced to be a single mother, she walked to work each day to make sure her family had all they needed. A few years passed, and she adopted her brother's daughter. Gladys never asked for help and was determined to raise her family on her own. Her life revolved around her children.

Gladys loved to sew and made all of her children's clothes. She could not afford to buy her own sewing machine, so she would walk to a neighbor's house to borrow hers when she could. Eventually, her children heard of a radio contest where the grand prize was a brand new sewing machine—they entered their mother, and she won a machine of her very own. She quickly put the new machine to use by sewing all of the choir robes for her church group.

Known for her amazing cooking, Gladys's specialties included fried chicken and fried fish. She often fed the entire neighborhood with her afternoon cookouts. Her gift of cooking was shared with many who enjoyed the warm meal and fellowship of neighbors.

Gladys had high expectations of her children. Today, they tell stories of how their mother would not settle for anything less than the best from each of them. They adore her for this gift that inspired their confidence and successes.

Although she was diagnosed with dementia and congestive heart failure, that's not how she will be remembered, that's not her story. Gladys's story is raising five successful children and too many grandchildren and great-grandchildren to count. She is facing the end of her life the way she has faced every other challenge or obstacle—with the gift of grace and dignity that has always inspired everyone around her.

The gifts Gladys has given to those around her cannot be counted or measured, but the world is a better place because she's in it.

Sonya with her patient, Alice

Thelma's Spirit

help anyone in need

Thelma Boudway was born in Waterbury, Connecticut, during the Great Depression. In 1948, she met the love of her life, Richard, and a year later gave birth to a daughter, Sonya. She was a nurturing mother to her only child, and she made it a priority to help anyone in need.

In 1966, Thelma went to work as a counselor for a juvenile girls' correctional facility. Her main goal was to help the girls turn their lives around. She always told her daughter that she couldn't help all of them, but the few she reached made her time worthwhile.

Thelma was diagnosed with kidney failure in 1980 and put on dialysis. One day at her apartment building, Thelma's neighbor asked her how she coped with being on kidney dialysis for four hours a day, three days a week. Thelma replied, "It is a lot like having a part-time job." The neighbor said, "But you aren't getting paid!" Thelma answered by saying, "I am because our Lord has given me time to live. Without kidney dialysis my life would be over." Thelma's positive spirit left her neighbor in awe.

While waiting for her dialysis treatment at the doctor's office, Thelma would ask other patients how they did over the weekend. If they expressed to her that they had not followed their diet, she would give them advice. Her main concern was their quality of life. She didn't want others to suffer. Because dialysis made the patients' mouths dry, Thelma oftentimes would bring them hard candies. Sometimes new patients even thought Thelma was the nurse or doctor because of her concern and care for them.

Thelma passed away in September of 1998 after 18 years on dialysis. She left behind in her daughter, Sonya, the same spirit to help others who are in need. Sonya and her two daughters, Monika and Robyn, volunteer for Covenant Hospice. Sonya says, "In each face I see, story I hear, and hand I hold, I remember how my mother always put someone else first."

Megan & Jim

Photo by Louise Couture Photography

Virginia's Ambition

the greatest strength and ambition anyone has ever known

At barely five feet tall and weighing just over 100 pounds, Virginia Murphy had the greatest strength and ambition anyone has ever known. She knew she could accomplish anything.

When she was just three months old, Virginia contracted polio, and as a result, had to be on crutches for the rest of her life. Yet, polio was not the only obstacle that she faced in her life: She also battled cancer, was in a serious car accident that left her having to learn how to walk all over again, was told she was unable to have children, and lived with braces and crutches. "My Nonnie never felt sorry for herself. She just pushed herself harder, conquering mountain after mountain," says her granddaughter, Megan.

Virginia's strength and determination were evident when, at 12, she traveled alone to Mobile from Slocomb, Alabama, on a Greyhound bus to have an operation. Later when she was old enough to go to college, she attended Troy State University and earned a teaching certificate in business. She also opened a floral shop at her home. It was the encouragement of Virginia's grandmother that gave her the belief that she could do anything that she wanted to…and she did.

Virginia taught shorthand, typing and business law at Coffee Springs High School where she met Jim Murphy. They fell deeply in love and were married in June of 1955. Just a year after their marriage, they were told that they could not have children, but in May of 1957 a huge surprise came—their first born, Marianne. Two years later, Virginia gave birth to their son, Don.

"When other people would have used this disability as an excuse not to do anything with life but to sit at home and vegetate, my Nonnie decided to push herself to success in whatever she pursued," says Megan. Once when Don was four years old, he was jumping off the top of their slide instead of sliding down the correct way. Jim was at work, so Virginia got a screwdriver and went outside and took the entire slide down by herself! Needless to say, Don didn't jump off the top of the slide anymore.

Virginia passed away in April of 2006. She will be remembered as a rock that many in her community and family leaned on for support.

Rosa Lee

Rosa Lee's Caregiver

cradling his mother in his arms

A parent's role is to provide and care for her child, but later in life roles are sometimes reversed and a child must care for their parent. This was the case for Johnny Scott who received a call in April of 1999 while living in Houston, Texas. His mother, Rosa Lee, was in very poor health. Upon hearing the news, Johnny immediately quit his job and moved back to Pensacola, Florida, to care for her.

As an only child, Johnny and his mother developed a very close relationship. "My mother taught me to treat everyone like I would like to be treated," says Johnny. Rosa Lee provided encouragement to Johnny as a child, telling him, "I want you to be somebody." That encouragement has stayed with him throughout his life.

When Rosa Lee became sick, it was Johnny's turn to be his mother's caregiver. He began making his mother her favorite foods to encourage her to eat. He cooked for her the way she had cooked for him when he was a little boy—fish and grits, cabbage and corned beef, and homemade biscuits.

A minister and pastor known for her dynamic speaking, Rosa Lee spent her life speaking at churches around the country and even traveled to the Holy Land for missionary work. Her life's lessons evolved from and revolved around her work: that you should love everyone regardless of the circumstances, that you should not make promises that you can't keep, and that God loves everyone equally.

At the end of Rosa Lee's life, Johnny found himself cradling his mother in his arms, the same way he was cradled when he was a baby. He would hold her frail face in his hands and, showing their closeness and connection, rub his nose with hers calling her his "sweetie." Johnny knows that his mother impacted many people throughout her life by the flowers and cards that arrived at her bedside—cards from Oregon, New York and even Newfoundland.

"I am very proud to be called Rosa Lee's son," Johnny says.

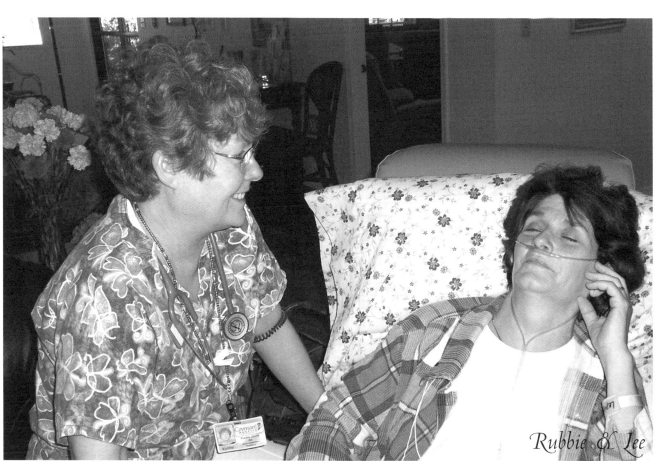

Rubbie & Lee

Lee's Rubbie

a true friend who will be there through thick and thin

Friends are there for you when you're in need, and once in a while, a person finds a true friend who will be there through thick and thin: a best friend. Lee and Rubbie found that friendship while working at Ralph's Grocery Store in California. "Lee and I just hit it off like that!" Rubbie says.

Throughout the years, Lee and Rubbie were inseparable. When Rubbie talks about their time together in California, her mischievous smile hints at the great adventures they shared.

Best friends for over 32 years, the women believe that their friendship has lasted so long because they are like two mismatched bookends. Lee is very direct, funny, organized and a wonderful decorator. Rubbie, on the other hand, is not direct, not so organized and a horrible decorator.

In 1990, Rubbie left California and headed to Pensacola, Florida, to be with her family. But, best friends are difficult to separate. A few years ago, Lee moved to Pensacola for work, and after being apart for over 10 years, the two bookends were back on the same shelf. "We were Lee and me all over again!" Rubbie exclaims.

Shortly after moving, tragedy struck: Lee was diagnosed with terminal lung cancer on her 49th birthday. Since Rubbie was a Covenant Hospice nurse and her best friend, she was the first person Lee called. Soon after the diagnosis, Lee was admitted to the Goldenberg Inpatient Residence. "I couldn't sleep at night until I knew she was able to be moved here and be taken care of by our staff," Rubbie says.

Today, the two act just like they did back at Ralph's Grocery Store in California—they tell jokes and make goofy faces—providing everybody a chance to witness their enduring friendship.

Photo by Meg Baisden Photography

Dressie Mae

Dressie Mae's Strength

common sense is the best thing you can have

Sitting upright in her chair and speaking in a quiet voice, Dressie Mae is the vision of a woman slightly weathered by her life experiences, trials and tribulations. Born in Wacissa, Florida, in 1913, Dressie Mae has experienced a lot in her life—from black men hung on trees to a cross burned on her lawn for renting her spare house to a white minister.

"I grew up in an area where there was a filling station and one little store," she recalls. Life was difficult then. Not only did Dressie Mae face challenges of racism and the Great Depression of the 1930s, she also faced the challenge of getting an education, which she overcame by earning her degree in cosmetology. Over the years, she won about six or seven trophies from hairstyle shows.

Dressie Mae and her husband Joseph married in her mother's kitchen and were together for ten years. She sees little comparison between her husband and men today. "Sometimes I think all the good men are gone. The men back in my days were nice, gentle and not demanding," she says, undoubtedly describing Joseph. The couple never had children, but many of the neighborhood kids became like their own. Not having children gave Dressie Mae the freedom to travel. She is proud to have flown 21 times and visited at least six states.

A strong woman, great motivator, and well-known political activist, Dressie Mae is a member of the Capital City Democratic Women's Club in Tallahassee, Florida, and was recently honored by the organization. They recognized her assistance in African American voter registration for arranging transportation to the polls and promoting freedom and equality for all.

Now in Covenant Hospice's care, Dressie Mae keeps her faith. "The best thing that happened to me in my life was when I acknowledged Jesus Christ," she says. Covenant Hospice helps her faith stay at the forefront of her life. "I sure like the man that comes and preaches and prays for me," she remarks, speaking of Chaplain Doug Mills.

Dressie Mae would like to leave these lessons with the world: "Common sense is the best thing you can have," she says. "Whatever God wants to happen will happen. You can't do anything about it. God says He will take care of you, and He's been taking care of me for a long time—92 years. Do the best you can in life, be kind, loving, and nice to people."

Jason & Melissa

Melissa's Faith

"I could not believe what I was hearing as I was becoming alert after the anesthesia from my lumpectomy: 'Melissa, you have cancer.' I kept thinking I must have misunderstood, I am really just groggy, my eyes are not even open yet, and I must still be in a deep sleep. The doctor must have made a mistake; maybe I just misunderstood what she was telling me. Am I still dreaming? As my eyes finally opened all the way, there standing over my bed was Jason, my new husband, and my dear friend Jasmine, both with tears in their eyes just looking at me. They were trying to smile and look as though they were not fearful, but I could tell they were just trying to be brave for my sake."

Melissa Hendrix experienced this and wrote these words in her book *It's All for Him*. Melissa was diagnosed with cancer at age 25, just two weeks after her marriage. For three and a half years, Melissa held strong to her faith and her favorite Bible verse, Romans 8:28. She found joy in her trial and gave powerful testimonies in church that made a tremendous impact on the congregation. Each time the cancer came back, Melissa knew that God had a plan and vision for her life. She led by example and allowed her joy to be a testimony to others even as she lost her hair and her health.

Melissa was featured in a Crestview, Florida, newspaper in a story telling of her struggle and faith. More stories soon followed regarding the release and dedication of her book to Heart of the Bride ministry. Since she could not have children, she wanted the proceeds from the book to be used by Heart of the Bride, a foundation that builds orphanages for children overseas.

Melissa's cancer eventually spread to her brain, but she remained steadfast with her faith in God.

"And we know that all things work together for good to them that love God, to them who are called according to His purpose." Romans 8:28

Margaret

Photo provided by the Malone family

Margaret's Heart

more than any volunteer has ever given

Ask folks in Foley or Gulf Shores, Alabama, what they know about Margaret Malone and you will hear many responses. Among them might be—

"She is the sweetest, dearest person I know."
"She has a heart of gold and loves her family."
"She is a true friend."
"She loves Mexican food."
"She is dedicated to her faith and her church."
"She has supported the arts for years."
"She brings a smile to my face every time I see her."
"She is a strong, giving woman."
"I want to be like Ms. Malone when I'm a 90-something-year-old."

Margaret is well known for her heart of gold. She volunteered for South Baldwin Regional Medical Center until she was 93 years old. When she 'retired,' the hospital hosted a celebration in her honor. They recognized her for volunteering more than 3,400 hours—more than any volunteer has ever given in the hospital's history.

Born in California in 1909, Margaret married William Cecil Malone in 1929. They had two children, Bob and Marilyn, whom Margaret proudly praises as "wonderful children who are both very successful and good people." Bob is very close to his mother. He loves that she never judges anyone and always accepts people as they are. Marilyn appreciates her mother's positive outlook on life and great sense of humor.

At age 97, Margaret is now in Covenant Hospice's care. She is a vibrant woman who continues to spend a great deal of time with her family. She is deeply loved by her children, grandchildren and great-grandchildren. They have milkshakes with her every Tuesday. Bob takes her to First Presbyterian Church in Foley every Sunday and they sit in 'their' seats on the second row. Bob makes sure his mother doesn't miss one word of the sermon. You will often see him leaning over to repeat the words directly in her ear.

Margaret's life lessons are simple: love God, never speak harshly or gossip, and always follow the golden rule. Her lessons have spread throughout her family, her church, and her community. They exemplify her faith, love and heart of gold.

Johnny

Photo by Autumn Fades Photography

Opal's Beauty

"Beautiful…the prettiest thing in Bay County," says Johnny Patronis about his beloved wife, Opal Messer Patronis. People always gravitated towards Opal and her magnetic spirit—her beauty inside and out. She was known for her strength and direction and as a compassionate woman, always pulling for the underdog.

Opal's strength would help carry her through a difficult time when an airplane accident left her a widow at the tender age of 25. In 1953, life took a positive turn when Opal met Johnny Patronis in Panama City, Florida. "When we first met, Opal would blush whenever I got close to her," Johnny recalls. He knew this was the first sign of her affection for him, and he couldn't have been happier.

After a 12-year courtship, Johnny and Opal married in 1965. While different in many ways, they also had a great deal in common—from boating to their love of travel to their compassion for the impoverished. "We were best friends," Johnny says. The years passed quickly but were filled with incredible adventures and clear, crisp memories. A vacation to London and Egypt proved to be the most exciting memory of all. "The Egyptians loved Opal's blonde hair. They would tell me that I'm a lucky man," Johnny remembers.

Throughout her life, Opal exercised and ate well to avoid diabetes, which ran in her family. So when cancer struck, the news came as a shock. Upon leaving the hospital for the last time, Johnny called Covenant Hospice. With the help of hospice staff, Johnny cared for Opal until she moved on from this life.

Looking back, Johnny chooses not to remember Opal's battle with cancer—the days where she was sick or couldn't leave her bed. Instead, he revisits a day from their adventure to Egypt, when his beautiful bride reluctantly hopped on the back of a camel in Cairo and proudly smiled as a camera captured the moment forever.

Opal impacted Johnny's life in many ways, but one of the most significant was imparting her gift of giving to friends and families in need, a gift which showed she was as beautiful on the inside as she was on the outside. Johnny has continued Opal's legacy by volunteering with and generously donating to Covenant Hospice.

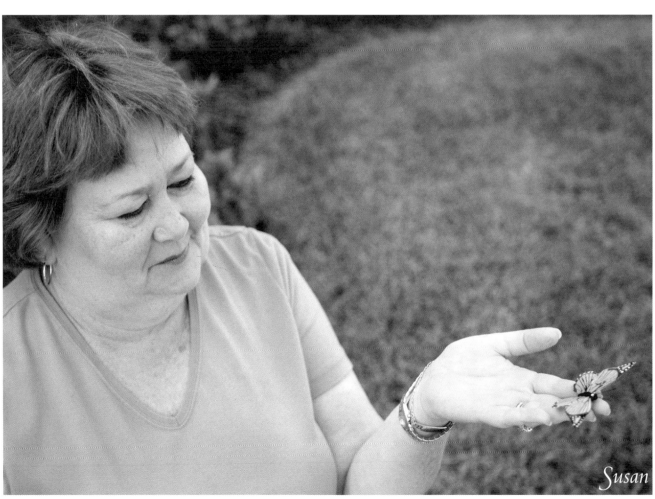

Photo by Look Who Just Blouin Photography

Susan

Larry's Flight

Susan and Larry met, fell in love, and spent 10 glorious years together. As a young couple living in Pensacola, Florida, they enjoyed the best of things in life, running a successful business and raising two beautiful children. Larry was always on the go with work, his family, and hobbies like hunting and fishing. The only dream Larry never realized was being a pilot: He wanted to fly.

When Larry became sick, Susan became his provider and caregiver. She insisted on taking her husband home to care for him. She had just heard of a new concept in end-of-life care —hospice—and jumped onboard. With the support of the Covenant Hospice team, Susan cared for her husband and even allowed their children to take part in decisions about his care. She believed that by including them, their father's passing would be less frightful and more believable for them. She was right. Aside from the medical assistance, a hospice volunteer also came once a week to take her kids for the day. Whether it was to a movie or out to get ice cream, the volunteer formed a bond with the children, and they looked forward to her visit each week.

Although this love story ended too soon, Susan thanks God for the time she had with Larry. He lived a good life and took her on a wonderful journey. Even at the end, he was a good man that looked out for the needs of others. Those that knew him still marvel at the bravery, strength and courage he displayed during his illness. He was positive of his place in Heaven and found peace in the journey to that destination.

For the past 16 years, Susan has been a dedicated Covenant Hospice staff member. She has seen the mission at work and calls her place there a calling.

Even though Larry never flew during his time on Earth, a friend did arrange for him to meet the Blue Angels and have a photo taken with them during his illness. And, Susan knows Larry is flying everyday in Heaven with his own two wings.

Angelica with her sisters

Photo by Gulf Reflections Studio

Angelica's Wish

In many ways, Angelica Venegas is just like any other seven-year-old girl. For fun, she loves to play Barbie with her former classmate and best friend, Brianna, and she especially loves to play with her very best friend and big sister, Andrea. Her hobbies also include drawing and coloring. She loves to show her friends and family that she loves them by creating cards. She's a great artist and won the first prize in coloring last February in school. Angelica is also a big fan of the Disney Channel—shows like *Dora the Explorer* and movies like *The Lion King* and *Shrek*. But, unlike most seven-year-olds, Angelica has End Stage Respiratory Disease and is under Covenant Hospice's care.

When a patient is admitted to Covenant Hospice, one of the first things the staff asks them is, "What are your goals or wishes that you want to accomplish?" Angelica had a definite answer and one big wish when she first arrived: for her mother and father to get married.

Angelica's wish came true on Mother's Day, 2006. With the help of the Fort Walton Beach, Florida, community and their caring donations of a photographer, florist, dresses, and other necessities, Angelica's parents were married on the beautiful, white sandy beaches of the Emerald Coast. Angelica and her sisters were a large part of the wedding: Angelica walked proudly as flower girl in a beautiful, yellow satin dress. "It was the most memorable day of my life!" she says. News of Angelica's wish spread all the way to the local media, and the special wedding day was featured in a newspaper article.

Angelica knows that wishes do come true and prayers are answered. Each day, family and friends surround Angelica with love and support. "I will never be happy in any celebration without my mother, father and big sister. They take good care of me, and they teach me everything I know," Angelica says. Together, she and her family continue to pray for her health and celebrate her life.

George

Photo by Gulf Reflections Studio

George's Attitude

not letting anything or anybody get me down

George believes that he is still alive because of his positive attitude about life. He is a self-taught computer repair man who gathers discarded computers, fixes them up, and gives them to neighbors and friends at cost. The neighbors on George's quiet street love and respect this man who gives so freely. Computers aren't his only area of expertise; several of the neighborhood lawn mowers are running today thanks to George's master mechanical ability, a gift which he attributes to his dad.

A native of Wheeling, West Virginia, George had a fragile childhood; he was susceptible to disease. His positive attitude and "having the best parents a person could ask for" were the two factors that got him to the point of gaining weight and strength and gave him the ability to do many different jobs in his life. He was a painter and construction worker, a roofer, a dishwasher, a Carnival "go-fer," a plumber, a teletype repairman in the Air Force, and a roustabout or seaman in the oil fields of the Gulf of Mexico. George was also a long-haul truck driver and served 24 years as a taxi cab driver in the Fort Walton Beach, Florida, area.

The happiest times of George's life were when his kids, two boys and two girls, and grandkids were born. He said, "It makes me happy to know that I have good kids, and it makes me love all kids all the more." George gets hugs and help from the neighborhood kids and has a close relationship with his seventeen-year-old niece, Theresa. George definitely has a love for young people, and they, in return, love him.

Cancer has been part of George's life for the past 22 years. He thinks that if he can deal with the pain, he will not die anytime soon. George commented that through Covenant Hospice he is getting the best care anyone could ask for. George says he is living life to the fullest now by "not letting anything or anybody get me down."

Marcia

Photo by Gulf Reflections Studio

Arthur's Mission

Arthur saw the need and filled it

Arthur Cormier and his wife, Marcia, enjoyed the good life. Married for 54 years with four children, five grandchildren and one great-grandchild, Marcia recalls, "We courted for eight years before we married. Young people just don't do that anymore," she says. Arthur and Marcia went to high school together in Massachusetts and graduated in 1945.

Arthur served his country in the Korean War before graduating from college with a B.S. in Electrical Engineering. He went on to Worcester State College to pursue an M.S. in Education, specializing in the Natural Sciences. Arthur was part of the nation's early space exploration program, working on the Interplanetary Monitoring Platform Satellite Project.

Arthur took his expertise and knowledge into the classroom, teaching Science, Biology and Physics at Grafton Senior High in Grafton, Massachusetts. Then after retiring, Arthur and Marcia served as missionaries to the Navajo Nation in Arizona for nearly four years. "What was supposed to be a two-week trip turned out to be a two-year stay," says Marcia of their initial visit to the Navajos. The couple took a short sabbatical before returning to the Navajo Nation for nearly two more years.

Arthur was a certified teacher, and the school on the reservation, Sun Valley Mission School, could not graduate the older children because they didn't have a teacher to teach upper level math. So, the need was there, and like so many other times, Arthur saw the need and filled it.

Arthur was dealt heart disease at the end of his life. "He was in Houston, and he just kept saying that he wanted to go home. He kept begging me to take him home, so we came home," Marcia says. Arthur's mission lives on in the children he taught, especially those from the Navajo Nation. "You'd like to think you're making a difference. We were just there to plant the seeds," says Marcia.

Lucy & Robert

Photo by Meg Baisden Photography

Robert's Passion

Robert Olen Butler, Sr. has lived his life doing what he loves with the woman he loves by his side. And, in a gentle voice, he's happy to share his story. Sitting comfortably in his recliner, Robert is the image of an aging professor: receding silver hair and distinguished bifocals crown his head. He is 87 years old.

"I was born in Granite City, Illinois, right across the Mississippi River from St. Louis, Missouri," Robert says. He met his wife, Lucy, in his hometown, and his eyes sparkle as he shares the memory of their first meeting. "She and her mother moved into an apartment next door to me and Dad after her father died. We went to high school together. Lucy was the prettiest and most popular girl in school."

After graduating from high school together, Lucy and Robert married in a simple ceremony in December of 1936.

Life after high school is a big part of Robert's story. "I wanted to go to college," says Robert, but "scholarships were not readily available to college students back then. If there was any financial help found, it was a one-time gift that ranged from 10 to 200 dollars." Robert feels lucky that Lucy was able to find a job out of school. "She took the Civil Service exam and got a job at Rock Island Arsenal in Rock Island, Illinois. That's how she supported the family and sent me to college," he says.

With Lucy's support, Robert earned a Bachelors of Fine Arts and a Masters of Fine Arts at St. Louis University. After graduation, he taught at the high school level and served as a professor of drama and speech at his alma mater. Later, he was awarded the distinction of Dean of the School of Drama and Speech. "The happiest time of my life has been spent doing a job that I love," he says.

Robert is also passionate about the time he dedicated to his country during World War II. "I served on the front line in the infantry," he says. After the war, Robert and Lucy welcomed their son, Robert, Jr. whom they affectionately call Bob Jr.

Bob Jr. shares his father's passion for the arts. He graduated from college with a focus on writing and has authored several novels. In 1991, Bob Jr. received the Pulitzer Prize for his fictional work entitled *A Good Scent from a Strange Mountain*, and he has worked on screenplays with celebrities like Robert Redford. As Robert shares this part of his story, the smile on his face conveys the overwhelming pride he feels for his son.

Robert sums his own story up well. "I came from practically nothing to become a university professor," he says. "Find the work that you really love to do. Work hard at it. Devote your time to it, and you will be successful."

Wilmer & Bud

Photo provided by the Knighton family

Wilmer's Bud

They say that a dog is a man's best friend. That certainly held true for Wilmer Knighton.

Wilmer grew up around farming, animals, and the outdoors. He worked on the family farm in Bluffton, Georgia, with his six siblings. He later bought a little land here and there for cattle farming after his time in the Army during World War II. Wilmer was an expert on cattle. People in the community would always come to him with questions or problems they were having with their cattle. They knew that Wilmer was honest and would always give them the right advice. Wilmer always told his son, Jim, that no matter how little a person had, he could work and have a good name. For Wilmer, nothing was more important than a person's good name.

In 2001, Wilmer moved to Jim's farm in Cowarts, Alabama. Wilmer had lost his wife in 1985 and retired from farming, so he spent his days with his constant companion, a terrier named Bud. Those two loved each other and were often found on the porch swing together.

When Wilmer's health began failing, his doctor referred him to Covenant Hospice. "Just as Daddy had a good eye for cows, he also had a good eye for the ladies, and he loved and thought the world of his nurse, Beth Peters," says Jim. Wilmer loved Beth, but the same couldn't be said for Bud.

Beth would drop by the house to check on Wilmer anytime he needed her, but Bud never looked Beth in the eye like most dogs do. "It was a joke around their house about Bud not liking me," Beth explains.

During Wilmer's final days, the family, including Bud, surrounded him, and something strange happened. Bud finally got close to Beth and looked her in the eyes. "It was almost like he was saying thank you for taking care of Wilmer," says Beth. When Wilmer died, Bud even followed the hearse for miles down the road.

Bud now lives with Jim, but he will always be Wilmer's best bud.

Christina

Photo provided by the Vautrot family

Christina's Moments

I was their only source of protection and security

Christina Dominique Jonviere Vautrot was only in her parents' care for a little over 13 months. However, Kathryn and Mills Vautrot still hold the love and inspiration that their daughter showed them while she was alive in their hearts and minds.

Born prematurely, Christina weighed only 1 lb. 6 oz. at birth. Like many premature infants, she was at great risk of developing liver and kidney cancer. Her parents' greatest fears were confirmed when their daughter developed fetal hypatoblastoma (liver cancer). "She was a sweet soul that I wanted to protect, yet she seemed to accept each situation with grace," said Kathryn. Christina's father, Mills, felt the same way, "She was the best and brightest thing that has happened so far in my life," he said.

Christina's daily activities became cherished memories for her parents. She loved bath time, blowing bubbles, foot rubs and would grin and wiggle when her daddy put on her socks. The little moments were magical. "The day after her birthday, she was in the hospital for chemotherapy. I was holding her and rocking her while watching *Read Between the Lions*. She was so content. It was like no one or nothing else existed but us," said Kathryn.

Their most fond memory of Christina is the way she would fall asleep on top of them and just "let go." Her father remembers that one night, when she came home after a long hospital stay, she snuggled into his shoulder and rested her head. "No one or nothing has ever let go like that, when I was their only source of protection and security. It was one of the most powerful and beautiful moments in my entire life."

Christina's short life taught her parents volumes. Her father says, "She taught me to believe, no matter what, to never give up, and to understand that there is something greater going on, and we all have our own role to play in it." Christina also taught her mother to live in the moment. "She taught me to love like there is no tomorrow, and to give tons of compassion for people who need extra tender care or who have special needs," said Kathryn.

Christina's parents surrounded her with love and made the most of all the little moments in life.

Harley

Photo by Gulf Reflections Studio

Harley's Fun

Harley Byron Campbell hails from Birmingham, Alabama, where his father owned a produce company and his mother was a homemaker. After attending Auburn University, he married the love of his life, Katherine, in 1938.

He and Katherine lived in Birmingham but vacationed in Fort Walton Beach, Florida. Mrs. Mooney, Fort Walton's first postmaster, rowed them over to see the property that would become their summer home. They placed an Army hut purchased from the salvage yard at Eglin Air Force Base on it and lived there like royalty for years. Since no road had been cut through, Harley and Capt. Eldredge, the first forester in Fort Walton Beach, spent two summers cutting a road where they thought it should go. It's now Eldredge Road.

Harley has been active in Square Dancing, Power Boat Squadron, Barbershoppers, Boy Scouts (his troop made a tape of his snoring since he didn't believe he'd kept everyone up all night) and the Model Railroad Club. His two Golden Retrievers, Cutty ("Sark") and Goldie, helped him build a model train track, complete with mountains and towns. Every time he'd try to run the trains, the dogs would put their paws up and knock them off the track. He loved those dogs!

Known for gathering up the neighborhood kids and his granddaughters just to make sure they got to see movies when they first came out, Harley also introduced his twin granddaughters to black and white musicals when they were three. To this day, *Bringing Up Baby* and *Singin' in the Rain* are two of their favorite movies. The twins call him Grandpa Bear because he loves to tease them that he is an old bear.

Covenant Hospice has the privilege of taking care of Harley now. You can hear him going down the hall in his wheelchair saying, "Beep beep." When you tell him what year it is he'll say, "That makes me 90 and that's too damn old." Harley keeps a smile on everyone's face with his singing. His favorite is, "Oh Lord, It's Hard to be Humble."

Even at 90 years young, Harley lives for the five F's in life: faith, family, friends, food, and—above all else—FUN.

Dorothy

Dorothy's Philanthropy

we make a life by what we give

Winston Churchill once said, "We make a living by what we do, but we make a life by what we give." Dorothy Cole from Marianna, Florida, agrees and has spent her life giving back to others.

Married to a dentist for 60 years, Dorothy feels the happiest time of her life was when she and her husband, Dr. Robert Cole—also known as Doc—offered free dental work in Honduras. "We went to do dental work in a small village that only had a church building and a river running through it," she says. During their time in the Honduran village, the couple slept on air mattresses, used a shower made of a papaya tree and washed their equipment in a tub with Pine-Sol®. Dorothy and Doc were able to help dozens in the poverty-stricken area.

Not only did they offer their services in Honduras, they also offered free dental work two times a year for 10 years in Piney Woods, Mississippi, and did mission work in Costa Rica and Guatemala.

But above all this philanthropy, Dorothy believes that her greatest personal accomplishment in life was organizing a Spanish club at Pascagoula High School so that Spanish classes could be taught there since they weren't offered when she was a student.

Dorothy has learned a lot in her 95 years, but the most important lesson she learned was that when you are giving service to others, you receive much more than you could ever give.

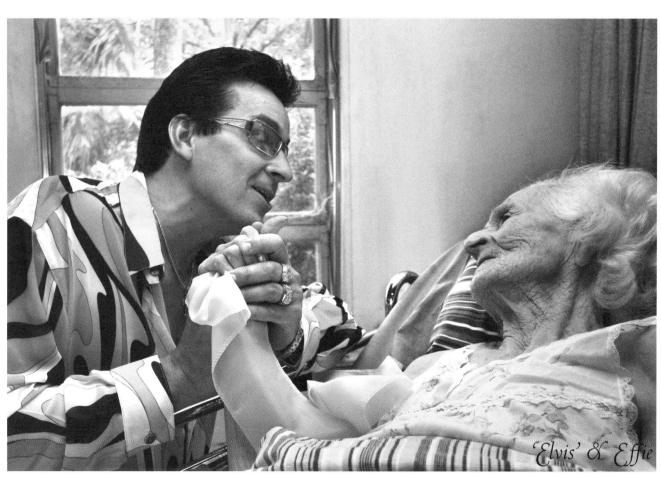

'Elvis' & Effie

Effie's Elvis

Leonard Bernstein once proclaimed Elvis Presley to be the greatest cultural force of the twentieth century. Effie Daffin, a life long Panama City, Florida, resident and avid Elvis admirer, couldn't agree more. In fact, Effie claims that Elvis had the "sweetest voice heaven ever made."

This tiny woman with silver hair and a sharp wit has loved Elvis since he burst onto the music scene in the 1950s. Although Effie is now in her nineties, bedridden, and under Covenant Hospice's care, her dream of seeing Elvis perform finally came true.

Arrangements were made for Gulf World entertainer and Elvis impersonator Todd Allen Herendeen to serenade Effie at her bedside. When Herendeen appeared at her house in full Elvis costume and crooned "Love Me Tender," her soulful blue eyes lit up like a giddy teenager's. "Oh, thank you, Jesus," she exclaimed. "I love you," she said, grasping Elvis's hand. Four generations of family members were there with Effie as Elvis sang to her.

Although Effie knew Herendeen wasn't the real Elvis, she was still overjoyed to see him. During his performance, she would periodically cry out: "Kiss me, Elvis, kiss me!"

"I was surprised at how enthusiastic and energetic she was," said Herendeen, who performs a Las Vegas style show at Gulf World Marine Park six nights a week. He sang several Elvis songs for Effie, ranging from classics like "Hound Dog" and "Blue Suede Shoes" to her favorite ballads and gospel songs like "Amazing Grace." "It was very touching for everyone," Herendeen said.

Several days after the surprise Elvis performance, Effie shared a bond with the real Elvis. As Elvis Presley fans across the world observed the anniversary of his death, she celebrated her 92nd birthday.

Dan

Hartward's Peace

he would often speak of his mother

Dan McMillan wants people to remember his friend Hartward White as a man who brought a smile to everyone's face with his quick wit and sense of humor.

A painter in the town of Brewton, Alabama, Hartward spent much of his life in the Merchant Marines and loved to tell stories of his travels. He lived a hard life and like most people, made his share of mistakes. In his later years, he was close to his family and to God. He learned lessons from both his good and his bad experiences and found peace as he grew into a better person.

Hartward loved to cook and fish. Occasionally he and his dog, Susie, would invite Dan and his family over for a great meal of his famous Camp Stew or Seafood Gumbo. He would tell some of the stories from his Merchant Marines days. Hartward also spoke often of his mother, who he had lived with and cared for at the end of her life. He shared his memories of her gentle spirit and how she read the Bible everyday. Dinner with Hartward was a real treat for Dan and his family.

Hartward was diagnosed with cancer, and eventually hospice became his family. Dan recalls, "The day he died, I happened to be in the room with him and the nurse. He had no living family. When he took his last breath, he seemed to be at peace and the room felt like all was well with Hartward," says Dan. "The nurse seemed to be Hartward's personal angel, there to help him die with dignity and comfort."

The Taylor Family

Pop's Harmony

no father and daughter were closer

During the summer between the ninth and tenth grade, Robin Taylor, who was only 16, lost her father. Two weeks into her tenth grade school year, her teacher Mr. Gregory O'Berry asked her to stay after class. He told her that he didn't know what was wrong, but that he could tell something was bothering her. He wanted her to know that he was there for her if she wanted to talk.

Robin told her teacher that her father had passed away over the summer and that her mother did not want her anymore. The next day, Mr. O'Berry told her that he and his wife Edith would be honored to have her come live with them.

Robin says that she was a bitter teenager, but they showed her unconditional love, generosity and absolute, selfless giving. "My life would be very different today without them," she says. Edith died in 1996 and when Gregory, or "Pop" as Robin calls him, was diagnosed with Alzheimer's in 1998, Robin and her three children became his caregivers.

Pop's motto in life was, "Together forever in perfect harmony." The motto, which was etched into his headstone, expressed his love for his family and his love of music. "His blood did not run in my veins, but no father and daughter were closer or loved each other more," says Robin. Once, when they were in the hospital, Robin was telling a nurse about how Gregory had taken her in and changed her life, and although he could not speak, Pop had tears streaming down his face. He had heard and understood everything.

Robin says that Pop lived life to the fullest, but that it was not about himself. "He always had a hug, smile or pat for everyone. He filled everyone around him with happiness and love." She says it was not what he got to do in his life, but what he got to do for others. "Pop blessed other people through his music and through his teaching. Seeing other people succeed or reach their goals is what he lived for," she said. "Pop lived life to the fullest by giving, helping and watching others grow."

Emmett's great-great-grandson Cody

Photo by Louise Couture Photography

Emmett's Faces

impacted the community, his country and his family

According to Tammy Fountain, her grandfather Emmett Lee Efurd was a man with many faces. Tammy cared for her grandfather as he battled Alzheimer's disease at his home in Hartford, Alabama. The time she spent with him was very precious to her. "Almost every minute was dedicated to giving back just a small portion of what he has given to me," she said.

In her grandfather, Tammy sees the face of a World War II veteran. Emmett enlisted at the young age of 18 with a buddy of his, who unfortunately did not make it back alive. "Photos I have of him in his dress uniform remind me of a little boy playing dress up in a man's world," said Tammy. He fought in the Battle of the Bulge where he was a calibrator on a tank. His Honorable Discharge lists battles and campaigns in Normandy, Northern France, Rhineland, Central Europe and Ardennes. He also received many decorations and citations, including the Purple Heart.

Tammy also sees the face of a policeman. After being approached by the Mayor of the City of Hartford, Emmett became the first certified police officer in Hartford history, a career change that he stayed with until he retired. "He was with the city for almost 30 years, and he wore his uniform proudly," said Tammy. Along with the face of the policeman came the face of a firefighter with the Hartford Volunteer Fire Department and a dedicated member of the Hartford Rescue Squad.

Another face she sees is that of a proud Mason, a past Master. "I was given the honor of pinning his 50 year pin on his pajama collar. This was a happy day for him and a proud one for me," said Tammy. Tammy's favorite face of Emmett's is that of a family man. She sees the face of a dedicated husband, father, grandfather, great-grandfather and great-great-grandfather.

"I miss him with every fiber of my being, but I am confident that he is rejoicing with my grandmother, other family members, old army buddies and friends," said Tammy of a man with many faces, who impacted the community, his country and his family.

"I guess the next face I'll see is that of an angel."

Rex and his family, Philip is to his far left

Photo provided by the Henderson family

Rex's Prayer

one of the those beautiful, creative flowerings of the spirit

In December 2004, Rex Henderson, a Covenant Hospice patient, was found on the floor beside his bed in the Henry County Nursing Home in Abbeville, Alabama. The nurse who discovered him assumed he had fallen, but in fact, he was on his knees in prayer. He was praying for his son, Philip, who was also under the care of Covenant Hospice 150 miles away in Panama City, Florida. He was terrified that his son would die before he got a chance to see him again.

Both father and son were extremely ill, but Rex, a retired minister, was the more stable of the two and longed to travel to say goodbye to his son. Covenant team members thought it was paramount that Rex and Philip get back together, if only for a few moments. The task of uniting them was going to be risky, difficult, and would require a great deal of cooperation between the nursing home and Covenant Hospice, but Rex's desire to see his son superceded all other considerations. After all, it was his wish.

Rex's daughter was anxious about taking the risk to drive Rex and her Mom to Panama City because of her father's condition. She saw him in his wheelchair with his head down and whispered in his ear. "Do you want to go see Philip?" she asked. When he replied, "I surely do," she knew they were doing the right thing. The trip went smoothly and when they arrived, Roger, Rex's other son, as well as Philip's daughter and other Covenant Hospice staff met them at Philip's home.

When Roger wheeled Rex into the family room, Philip was able to smile and wink before lapsing back to sleep. Roger placed Rex's hand on Philip's hand and heard Rex whisper, "Come on, boy, let's go fishing." "It was one of those beautiful, creative flowerings of the spirit we are sometimes blessed to witness," the nurse said. The love that flowed from father to son encompassed everyone in the room and felt like a rich and spontaneous gift. Rex and Philip had spent many days fishing together when Philip was growing up. It was a dear passion they both shared.

When Rex returned to Henry County Nursing Home, a Covenant Hospice chaplain was waiting to have prayer with him. In the hours following the farewell visit, both men lapsed into unconsciousness. Philip passed away January 24, 2005 and Rex on January 25, 2005, just 17 hours apart.

The families express confidence that Rex and Philip are again united, fishing together where the water is calm and the fish are leaping.

Lucy and her family

Photo by Ryan Lee Caver

Lucy's Exuberance

take advantage of every minute

Lucille Brunson, or Lucy as many knew her, was not going to give in quickly to anything, including cancer. She was too strong, too stalwart and too totally determined to take advantage of every minute spent with all that she loved. She lived life to the fullest every moment of every day.

Lucy loved so many things in life, from swing dancing to beautiful flowers to wild animal prints to that delicious Southern cooking. Many of those around Foley, Alabama, especially remember her scrumptious peach cobbler.

Lucy was a fashionable woman and loved to decorate her outfits with crazy pins and necklaces. She adored bright red fingernail polish and matching toenail polish. She loved pretty pink lingerie and wonderful wigs she used when she lost all of her hair from chemotherapy.

When things were at the lowest for Lucy, she always had a way of brightening the day. As in the time when her daughter, Zana, almost dropped her on her head while trying to give her a bath. "It'll be OK," Lucy remarked, "even if I have to die dirty." Lucy was always lifting the spirits of those around her with a smile or joke, remaining steadfast for her friends in chemotherapy and building new relationships with the staff and volunteers at Covenant Hospice.

The ultimate acknowledgement of Lucy's impact on the world can be seen by the tremendous love that was given to her in return.

Totally unique, totally her own, Lucy totally impacted the world with her exuberance.

Photo by Gulf Reflections Studio

Wayne & JoAnn

JoAnn & Wayne's Foundation

it's gotta be each of you giving 100%

Wayne and JoAnn Gardner will soon celebrate their 49th wedding anniversary. They met at a hole-in-the-wall juke joint called the Cotton Club in West Memphis, Arkansas. Wayne was a Marine stationed in Memphis for training. JoAnn was out celebrating a friend's graduation from high school with a group of girlfriends. "As soon as that group of girls walked into the club," says Wayne, "I elbowed one of my buddies in the ribs and told them 'the tall one's mine.'" JoAnn was about 5'10" back then, and in heels, she was six feet tall and gorgeous. Wayne reminisces, "I'll never forget the way she looked that night…the dress she wore and everything." Wayne and JoAnn kept the pretty, pale aqua dress she wore.

They dated mostly on the porch of her parent's house, and it was at the house, three months later, that JoAnn proposed. Wayne remembers, "She came into the living room one night, jumped into my lap on the couch and said: 'Why don't we get married?'"

The day they married was one of the proudest moments of Wayne's life. "We became one August 2, 1957," he says. Wayne's philosophy on marriage is that it isn't 50/50—"it's gotta be each of you giving 100% to make it work."

Wayne and JoAnn have never had a fight in 49 years of marriage and have three children: Stephen, Theresa and Kayren, and a granddaughter, Kristen, whom they have raised as well. All of their children live nearby.

JoAnn was a tidy homemaker for many years before her illness, multiple sclerosis, which keeps her bedridden. She says, "The best thing about my life today is my husband. He's very good to me. He waits on me hand and foot."

If you visit Wayne and JoAnn today you will notice a little hand-carved stool with a heart on top. Wayne made it for JoAnn so that she could get into her bed more easily. They say it signifies the strength of a love built on a sturdy foundation.

Contributing Photographers

Carmen's Custom Framing and Photography

Carmen Jones has been working with photography since she was a small child. Her passion for photography came after her twin nephews were born in 1996. After working with kids and nonprofit organizations extensively, Carmen decided to follow her passion and began photographing kids and families in their natural form, which made *Faces of Life* an excellent fit. Carmen operates her custom framing and photography business from her home in Pensacola, Florida. 850-432-7563, carmensandiego18@bellsouth.net

Autumn Fades Photography

Autumn Fades Photography is owned and operated by photographer Dustin Bryson. He has been shooting professionally for nine years and has run Autumn Fades from Seattle, Washington; Columbus, Ohio and now Panama City, Florida. His work has been featured in newspapers, magazines, coffee table books, and on television and Web sites. While his most well known work comes from shooting promotional and live shots for bands, Dustin's passion is capturing honest moments, and human reactions as they happen. Dustin is also the founder of a photographers and filmmakers missions ministry called Agony & Angels that provides documentary film and docutography to non-profit organizations helping people around the world. 850-960-0299, www.autumnfades.com

Mattox Studio

Mattox Studio is owned and operated by Estal and Wanda Mattox. Estal is a Certified Master Photographer and has also been the recipient of the Florida Degree of Photographic Excellence. They have been in the photography business for over 10 years. Their studio is located in Graceville, Florida. Estal and Wanda work together in the studio to create portraits for children, families, high school seniors and weddings. They feel that it is a privilege to create memories that will last a lifetime. 850-263-2738, www.mattoxstudio.com

Gulf Reflections Studio

Gulf Reflections Studio, Inc. has been serving their community for over 20 years. Co-owners Marcia and Michael Wright Reynolds have created thousands of lasting portrait memories. Marcia has a lifetime of photography experience and opened Gulf Reflections Studio in Fort Walton Beach in August 1985. Marcia received a Masters of Photography Degree in 1998 from the Professional Photographers of America. She earned a Craftsman degree from PPA, equivalent to a Doctorate degree, in 2003. She is currently one of the number one Master Craftsman Photographers in the southern United States of America. Michael and Marcia are both Certified Professional Photographers and Gulf Reflections Studio is the only studio on the Gulf Coast with two Certified Photographers. They both love photography and enjoy sharing their talents with their customers. 850-863-2288, www.gulfreflections.com

Contributing Photographers

Look Who Just Blouin Photography

Trista Blouin specializes in artistic child portraiture of residents and visitors along the Emerald Coast. She received her formal photographic training while in her home state of Minnesota, but has learned most of what she knows through years of experiencing and understanding how children view the world. She believes that an artful, meaningful photograph comes about only through an understanding of the individual's unique facets, a process that takes time and patience. Her own spirit has been uplifted through working with the *Faces of Life* participants. Each person has shown her just how rich each breath can be. 850-712-1513, www.lookwhojustblouin.com

Louise Couture Photography

Louise Couture Photography is a small studio with big service and big quality. Combining her study and practice of professional photography, Louise's art in classic portraiture with a photojournalistic and natural style allows you to express your true beautiful self through her lens. She specializes in weddings, senior photos, and once-in-a-lifetime celebrations. 334-886-3710, www.lcouturephoto.com

Meg Baisden Photography

Meg Baisden Photography is a dynamic husband and wife photography team that offers contemporary wedding photography to the Gulf Coast and beyond. Specializing in artistic documentary wedding coverage for the modern bride and groom, Meg and Charles Baisden are award-winning members of the highly esteemed Wedding Photojournalist Association (WPJA) and Wedding and Portrait Photographers International (WPPI). 850-455-7724, www.megphoto.com

RE: Productions

Photographer Robert Evers of Andalusia, Alabama, is the owner of RE: Productions which specializes in professional wedding, commercial, and event photography and cinematography. He holds a B.A. in Telecommunications and Film and an MA in Advertising and Public Relations from the University of Alabama. He is a former associate producer with the University of Alabama Center for Public Television and is a veteran of the US Marine Corps. 334-222-2727, www.roberteversprod.com

Faces of Life Legacy Gifts

To celebrate the lives of our families and friends, we give…

In Memory of	Given By
Dorothy Cole	Daniel & Barbara Cole
Wallace Cooey	Thelma Cooey
Nell G. Odom	Charles A. Lancaster
Rosa Lee Scott	The Scott Family
Opal R. Stanley	Windom Stanley
Christina Dominique Jonviere Vautrot	G. Mills & Kathryn Vautrot
Judith Woods	David Woods

In Honor of the Covenant Hospice Staff and Volunteers…

Brown Helicopter, Inc.
Compass Bank
Pace, Florida, Wal-Mart #990

Letter from the President & CEO

A seven-year-old boy asked his grandmother what compassion meant. Her husband of 42 years had recently passed away under the care of Covenant Hospice. She hadn't said much since his death. She sat, reflecting on her grandson's question. He asked again. She replied, "Compassion is remembering the good things about Grandpa, not just remembering his illness. Compassion is the way he interacted with his family and his friends. Compassion is the way Grandpa lived every day. Compassion is the way he died."

After hearing this story, I thought about the legacy the gentlemen left behind. I also thought about my own life and what type of legacy I might leave behind.

Covenant Hospice has cared for more than 37,500 patients over the past 23 years. We are humbled and honored to have had the opportunity to be a part of so many lives. With this book, we are presenting you a small number of these courageous and accomplished people. Our hope is that you will find something compelling about them that reflects in your own life.

I cannot imagine anything more personally and professionally fulfilling than being involved with hospice and the end-of-life journey. I applaud you for reading this book and looking into the many extraordinary *Faces of Life*.

Dale O. Knee
President & CEO
Covenant Hospice

To order additional copies of this book, visit www.covenanthospice.org or call (850) 433-2155.